To Crysta ♡

SO-ADU-561

THE
SUPERB
WOMAN

IT'S ALL ABOUT THE **BE**

Be well
Janet M. Neal

Janet M. Neal

NEW YORK

LONDON • NASHVILLE • MELBOURNE • VANCOUVER

THE SUPERBWOMAN
It's All About the BE

Published in New York, New York, by Morgan James Publishing. Morgan James is a trademark of Morgan James, LLC. www.MorganJamesPublishing.com

The Morgan James Speakers Group can bring authors to your live event. For more information or to book an event visit The Morgan James Speakers Group at www.TheMorganJamesSpeakersGroup.com.

ISBN 9781683504689 paperback
ISBN 9781683504696 eBook
Library of Congress Control Number: 2017902479

Cover and Interior Design by:
Chris Treccani
3 Dog Creative
www.3dogcreative.net

In an effort to support local communities, raise awareness and funds, Morgan James Publishing donates a percentage of all book sales for the life of each book to Habitat for Humanity Peninsula and Greater Williamsburg.

Get involved today! Visit
www.MorganJamesBuilds.com

To my grandmother, Carol Potter, and my mother,
Barbara MacMeekin –
Superbwomen who helped me find my path

CONTENTS

CHAPTER 1:
SHE'S GOT IT ALL

They walked into the auditorium, confident and proud: Nubian princesses, Anglo-Saxon queens, Greek goddesses—alone, in pairs, or in a group, chatting excitedly. Bea stared at their eager faces from her place at the registration desk, wondering why these strong women needed to attend an empowerment conference. *I should be the one taking this, not them*, she thought, as she smiled and handed a packet to the next attendee. In a moment they would be settled in the auditorium, ready to take in the cherished wisdom of today's speaker, a media icon who had it all. Bea was hoping her work responsibilities wouldn't keep her from listening in on a bit of the speech. *Boy*, she thought, *I really need it!*

A buzzing from the phone stashed in her pocket jolted Bea back to reality. She stole a glance to see who was calling. It was Abigail's school—not a good sign. Fortunately, her duties were winding down, and she asked her coworker to cover her position while she scurried off to find a quiet corner to return the call.

"Hi, this is Ms. Parker returning your call," Bea warily announced to the school secretary.

"Oh, hello, Ms. Parker. Abigail is here and needs to talk to you." Bea's mind raced with myriad reasons why her 12-year-old daughter was calling during school. *Was she sick? No, I don't remember her looking sick. Was she in trouble? Hmm, unlikely, but there was always a first time. Was she hurt? Hope not. Did she forget something?...*

Before she could run through what was missing, Abby interjected. "Hi Mom. I forgot to bring my permission slip for the field trip, and I need it today. Can you bring it over?" Bea pictured the unsigned slip sitting on the kitchen counter—one more thing she forgot to do last night!

"Oh, sweetie, I can't, I'm working a conference today."

"But Moooommmmmm... I HAVE to have it!" She could tell Abby was on the verge of tears and tried hard to come up with a solution in the moment. There was no way she could leave her work, today of all days, but maybe there was a workaround.

"Listen, Abby, it will be OK. Put Mrs. Spears back on the phone, OK?"

"Fine!" was the reply, probably garnished with an eye roll for good measure.

"Hi, Mrs. Spears. You probably heard that, but the permission slip is at home, and I can't get there until after school. Is there any way you can take a verbal OK from me now, and I'll bring it later when I pick Abigail up?" A brief hesitation made Bea wonder if Mrs. Spears was doing an eye roll as well.

"I guess that would be acceptable," she answered. "Please do not forget it this evening, though. We'll be here until 4 p.m."

Four p.m.? Great, Bea thought, *I'll have to leave early. Again.* "Fine, I'll be sure to be there by then. Thank you for your help! Can you please put Abigail back on the phone for a minute? Thanks!"

"What?" Abby answered. Now it was Bea's turn to roll her eyes. Some days...

"Listen, I just wanted to say it is OK, and I'll bring the slip later. I'll pick you up by 4 tonight... I know, it's early. I have to run, sweetie—have a fun trip!"

"OK, thanks, Mom!" came the cheery reply.

Bea sighed. Well, pre-teens' moods were certainly changeable! Her 9-year-old-son, Max, may be full of energy, she thought, but thank goodness she still had a few years before he hit this phase as well!

Bea closed her phone and made her way back to the lobby. As she passed the auditorium door, she paused, then snuck inside to catch a few moments of the talk. She'd seen the speaker on television, but never in person before. Dana Meadows was a dynamic woman who radiated a calm strength, and her words had the crowd mesmerized. Bea looked at the women in the audience, nodding their heads in agreement to what was being said, and realized that something had changed. No longer were these the confident women she'd seen a few moments before. Their demeanor was now one of... what was the word? Bea struggled to think of what it was she was witnessing. Suddenly it hit her: They were looking and acting a lot like her, a stressed-out, overwhelmed, guilt-ridden woman, trying to do it all. She couldn't believe it. They had no idea how powerful they really were! Could that possibly be true for her as well? As Bea contemplated this new idea, she was jostled back to reality by an opening door. She shook off the thoughts and turned to get back to work. Best to leave that kind of thinking for another day!

That evening, after the kids were fed, homework was done, and the dog was walked, Bea finally had some alone time. The thoughts from that morning came back to her: What was it that made some women really strong and confident? Why did some appear to be that way at times but at other times did not? And was it possible for her to ever feel as confident as Dana Meadows? She decided it was time to find out.

CHAPTER 2:
HOW DOES SHE DO IT?

Bea glanced at the clock and sighed. Where had the morning gone? Her mind raced to calculate how much time before her next meeting. *Well, I think I can still squeeze it in if I give up lunch... again,* she thought, weighing the pros and cons of her options. A glance at her chipped nails secured her decision. *Guess I'll eat on the way,* she thought, as she grabbed a bag of chips and her purse and left for the nail salon.

The bells on the salon door jingled as she opened it to find a full house. She was contemplating her options when the manicurist in the back, lost in conversation with her client, looked up and, with a smile of recognition, waved her over. Bea flashed a weak smile and headed apologetically through the crowded salon in her direction.

"Well, hey, Sugar! I didn't think I'd see you until Friday!" the manicurist said as Bea approached her.

"Hey, Velma. Yes, well, I have a bit of an emergency here. I have a big meeting coming up this afternoon and, well..." She flashed her chipped nails into Velma's line of sight. "Do you think you can fit me in? So sorry..."

"Oh, I should say you do! Now, don't fret—we'll just take care of you now. Mary, sweetheart, can you be a dear and take care of Portia here for me? We have a real emergency on our hands here. So to speak!" Velma laughed. "You just have to laugh, don't you?! Here, Sugar, just sit down and let Velma have a look at this mess."

Bea sat down, relieved to have a few minutes to relax and let Velma do her magic.

"So, tell me—what's new in that life of yours?" Velma asked.

"Not much," Bea began, and then offered, "although we did produce the Dana Meadows event this week."

"You don't say! Oh, I just love her: Awareness, Acceptance, Abundance. She just has it all, doesn't she? That must have been something to see!"

"Well, I actually didn't see much of it—working at it, you know." Bea noted.

"Oh, but honey, just being there in the same space with her—some of that magic must have rubbed off!

Honestly, you have such an exciting life!" Velma said, shaking her head.

Bea scoffed. "Oh yeah, right! But, you are right about something: Dana Meadows does have some kind of magic. How do you think she does it?"

"Money. She has more money than God, you know. She can just pay people to do everything for her. Why, I read in my papers that she..."

Bea knew where this was going and interjected, "Yes, that certainly doesn't hurt, but here's the thing. I noticed that there were a LOT of women who came to this event who seemed to have it altogether as well. And I know they aren't all as rich as her. How is that? And, what was even more interesting was that they didn't even seem to know how, um, powerful they were. It just baffled me."

"Sugar, women are always doing that—giving away what they got and not seeing how amazing they truly are. I see it every day! Mercy, look at you! You are doing it all, what with that job of yours, and here you are raising those two babies all by your lonesome. Velma sees it!"

Bea smiled. "And this is why I keep coming to you, Velma. You're the best."

Velma nodded, "You're darn tooting right! Well, it's like Dana says, Awareness, Acceptance, Abundance. I've got that awareness down, and I'll be grateful to accept some abundance, too!" she added with a wink.

"I'm right there with you on that!" Bea added. "Do you really believe that stuff... what she says? You don't think it's some New Age mumbo jumbo?"

"Sugar, if it gets me the life that Dana has, I'm in. I don't care who says it! But seriously, look at her—she's got the life! Like I said, she's got the magic. I believe her. You should listen to her! Now, dip your hand in here, Sugar."

Bea thought about it. There was something about Dana that just radiated confidence. And it wasn't the money. It was coming from within—a sense of serenity and contentment that Bea longed for. Maybe Velma was right. Maybe there was something to it. Maybe it was worth a try.

"You know, you may be right," Bea noted. "How do you think someone would get started on trying to 'be like Dana'?"

"Well, like she says, start with the Awareness. The Good Lord knows I am blessed to see ladies every day. Some of them are the good eggs, like you. Others, well, let's just say they don't have a lick of sense. I say talk to people! You'll figure out who is the real deal and who is nothing but a cheap suit pretty darn quick. Why, in no time, you'll be owning this place!" Velma smiled and added, "Then you can thank me by giving me a nice fat retirement check!"

Bea laughed. "You got it, Velma. Maybe I'll just buy you your own place: Velma's Nails."

"Don't you laugh, now. You listen to Velma—you got something there! OK, let me have a look-see. There—you are as pretty as a picture again. Now go on and scoot back to that cushy job of yours!"

"Thanks, Velma. You're a life saver!" Bea said as she stood to leave.

"Yes indeedy," she answered. "Now scoot! You got big things to do!"

CHAPTER 3:
IN SEARCH OF THE QUEEN BEE

Bea sat on the metal bleachers with the other moms waiting to pick up their sons from soccer practice. It was interesting, Bea noted, how the group fell into two camps: the stay-at-home moms who were huddled together talking, and the working moms, sitting somewhat by themselves, engrossed in their cellphones. Bea reflected on her conversation earlier in the week with Velma. Velma had suggested that it starts with awareness. Bea looked around. Here were women who, on the outside, seemed to have it all, but there were only a few who had "it." What was it about them? Why did they have this presence and the others didn't?

Bea was lost in thought when she was brought back to reality by a voice saying, "Mind if I join you?" It was her neighbor, Nancy.

"Oh, hi Nancy—I didn't even see you there! Guess I was somewhere else!" Bea said.

"Yes, you looked a little preoccupied! Everything OK?" Nancy answered as she spread a blanket on the cold metal seat. "I can't believe how cold it is getting!"

"I know—smart of you to think of that blanket! And yes, I'm fine. I was just thinking about a conversation I had earlier in the week."

"Must have been a good one!" Nancy laughed.

"Actually, it really has me thinking. Let me ask you: You know Dana Meadows, right?"

"Well, not personally, but of course. You were talking to her?!" Nancy asked.

"Oh, heavens no. I wish. No, I was mentioning to my manicurist that we put on a workshop that she spoke at last week, and how I want to be like Dana when I grow up. How do you think she does it?" Bea asked.

"Well, I think it's a combination of things. I think she is truly blessed, but I also think she's worked for it. Worked on herself, that is. I think she practices what she preaches. You know, that 'Awareness, Acceptance, Abundance' stuff?"

"Do you believe in that?" Bea asked.

"Yeah, I think there is something to it. Sounds like this has really got you thinking!" Nancy answered.

"It really has. I don't know... I'd really like to find a way to be more like her. You know, comfortable in my own skin." Bea answered.

"You're not?" Nancy asked. "You could have fooled me!"

"Well, that's the thing. I've been fooling a lot of people, including myself, for a long time. I think it's time I did something about it. I'm just not sure how to start. Velma, my manicurist, told me to just start by talking to other women and seeing what they think. So I guess I just did!" Bea laughed.

Nancy smiled. "She sounds like a wise woman! That's a great idea! I don't know about you, but these days I need to write everything down or it is gone! Maybe you could keep a journal or something."

"Great idea! Make it like a real project! See, Velma was on to something with this talking to other women! Thanks!" Bea said.

"No problem. Just mention me to Dana when you two are talking about this!" Nancy smiled.

"Deal!" Bea joked.

That night, after dinner was made and served, homework done, laundry folded and the kids were finally settled in their rooms, Bea rummaged through her cupboards looking for something on which to collect her thoughts. As she was about to call it a night, she spied a package, wrapped loosely in tissue paper. It looked to be a book of some sort. Curious, Bea pulled it out and unwrapped it. It was a beautiful blank book—a journal. On the cover was a bee, adorned with a crown. Bea stared at it. She had no idea where it came from or how long it had been there. It seemed almost magical to have found it.

Guess this was meant to "bee," she said to herself. *Or meant for Bea, I guess. A Queen Bee. Perfect!* She got into bed and opened the book, excited to start her journey.

Let's see, she thought. *How do I begin? Well, I guess maybe by defining what I am looking for. Maybe I'll call her "The Queen Bee."* And she began writing:

In Search of The Queen Bee
Who She Is and How She Got There

On the following page she wrote:

Who is a Queen Bee?
Dana Meadows

Qualities of a Queen Bee:

comfortable in own skin

positive energy

not concerned about what others think

doing amazing things

confident

successful

And then she wrote Dana Meadows' advice:

Awareness

Acceptance

Abundance

Bea took a moment to consider all of this. She was starting on the Awareness part, as Velma suggested, by talking to other women to get their ideas. Who did she know that fit the Queen Bee criteria, she wondered? Bea closed the journal and went to sleep, excited to see where this new adventure would take her.

CHAPTER 4:
GETTING TO KNOW YOU

Bea glanced at the clock. 4:30. "Shoot!" she said, "I'm going to miss Max's game completely if I don't get out of here soon!" She made a quick mental note of what absolutely had to get out today and put the other papers in her desk. There would be plenty more to do tomorrow, but right now she had traffic to beat.

A dash to the train, some more emails on the trip, and then a quick drive to the soccer field. Whew! It looked like it had just started. Bea grabbed her chair out of the trunk and wove her way towards the field. She had learned the hard way that bringing your own seating was a lot easier and more comfortable than trying to make your way up the cold metal bleachers—in heels. She looked for an open spot to plant her chair and spied one next to another mom, Kelly White.

"Hey Kelly," she said, "mind if I join you?"

"Well, hi there, stranger!" Kelly answered. "Pull up a seat and tell me what's new."

Bea opened the seat and plopped down into it with a sigh. "Whew. What traffic today! Glad I made it before it was over!" She glanced over at Kelly, who was dressed in jeans and a sweater. "You look comfortable—did you get out of work early?"

Kelly smiled. "I'm not working anymore."

This kind of news was always confusing to Bea. Was this good news or bad? What does one say to this proclamation? She decided to take the cautious path. "Congratulations... I guess?"

Kelly laughed. "Yes, it was my choice. And yes, I'm really happy with my decision."

Bea was startled. Kelly had been an up-and-coming executive with a well-known investment firm. She was known in the industry as a power broker and was garnering national attention for her deal-making abilities. "Wow. I... I don't know what to say! What a shock! How did this all come about, if you don't mind my asking."

"You're not the only one who was surprised by it. I kinda surprised myself!" Kelly continued, "You know, in hindsight I realized that I'd been moving towards this point for quite a while, but I was so caught up in the rat race that I couldn't see it. Or see that I needed it. You know how that is?"

Bea nodded. "I sure do. But I'm so curious as to how you had the courage to just quit! I could never do that! Besides, I'd have no idea what I'd do. How did you do it?"

Kelly shook her head. "Oh I hear you—I NEVER thought I would do this. But like I said, it kinda crept up on me. I was working 80 to 100 hours per week, flying around the world, meeting all these high-power people. It was a rush—very exciting. Well, in the beginning it was. Then, after the kids came, the guilt started to creep in, but I was pretty good at pushing that away. Or so I thought. Gradually, little things started to bother me—the wheel on my suitcase breaking, not having my dry cleaning ready, not being able to connect to wifi—all in all, not big deals, but I was having BIG reactions to them. I lost all patience at work, and my poor husband took the brunt of what spilled over to home. It got so bad that my boss 'suggested' I take a few weeks off with the family. Of course, I thought that was a sexist statement and tried to refuse. But then he took me aside and pointed out that I was not being as effective as I usually was, and that he was actually concerned about me, so I relented."

"Yikes," Bea said. "That must have stung."

"Oh, it sure did," Kelly remarked. "But in hindsight he really did me a favor. We took two weeks and went to our house on the island, and I made a vow to unplug. OMG—have you ever tried to do that?! It was like going through withdrawal!"

"I don't know if I could do it," Bea said.

"Well, I didn't think I could, either, but I told my family about it, and they were MORE than happy to help keep me honest! But anyway, during those two weeks, I did nothing except what felt good. I read books for fun, I swam, I biked, I ran. I played games with the kids. I sat around and did NOTHING. It was heaven... well, the second week was heaven. The first was still a little nerve-wracking! And then when I got back to work after that, a funny thing happened to me. I had more patience in some ways, but in others, I had less."

"What do you mean?"

"Well, I was a nicer person, and those little things didn't bug me like they used to. But it was the work I was doing. It wasn't making me happy. Actually, what those two weeks did for me was to remind me what 'happy' felt like and to remind me that I deserved to feel happy. It was like I got some sort of 'altitude' on my life and could see the kind of example I was leaving for my kids. It was all about MORE—more money, more power, more STUFF. And none of it was making me happy. It was like I woke up and looked around and saw that I had climbed to the top of the ladder… but it was the wrong ladder! I knew then that I had to leave."

"Wow. That's incredible! What an experience! So what are you doing now?"

"Well, it's been an adjustment for everyone, but I find that the more I am learning to be self-aware, the better a partner and mother I am. By figuring out what makes me happy, and then doing it, I am a better person to be around, I'm making better decisions, and hopefully, I'm being a better role model to my kids. Quitting your job with nothing planned to take its place is definitely not for everyone, but it was for me. I couldn't be happier!"

"Well, you look fabulous! Thanks so much for telling me your story! Sounds like self-awareness is the way to go!" Bea noted.

"Who knew?" Kelly added with a laugh.

That evening, Bea took out her journal and thought about her conversation with Kelly. Her willingness to really look at her life and what made her happy was inspiring. Bea made a notation on her chart:

AWARENESS

Self-awareness: take a look at what makes
you happy

ACCEPTANCE

ABUNDANCE

Tomorrow was another day—and Bea felt strangely
confident that more lessons were on the way!

CHAPTER 5:
BECOMING DANA-LIKE

Bea walked into the break room at work to find her boss, Rhonda, sipping a coffee. "Hey, Rhonda, how was the weekend? Wasn't last weekend the weekend you guys were getting away?" Bea had worked with and for Rhonda for such a long time that their relationship had more of a feel of a friendship, rather than a typical boss-employee one.

Rhonda just shook her head. "Yes, well, Bill had to work again, so we had to postpone it." She noticed Bea's look and replied, "Oh, it's OK. I was really tired anyway—you know what last week was like!"

Bea only partially believed her. "Yes, it was one for the record books, but really? You were so looking forward to it! If he couldn't go, couldn't you ask a friend—or your sister?"

"Oh, gosh, no," Rhonda said. "Bill would be very disappointed to miss it. No, it's OK. We'll find another time. And how about you? Anything exciting?"

"Me? Nah. Just kid things. At least you still have some semblance of a life! I dream of the day I actually have a Saturday to myself!" Bea stirred her coffee, lost in that thought.

"Well, at least you have those kids. I think that would be so much fun to do all those 'Mom things,' like watching them play sports, reading them stories, tucking them in at night..."

"Spoken like someone who doesn't have any kids! I'll be glad to lend a couple to you!" Bea retorted. "You know, you still have time for one of your own..." It was a subject they had talked about frequently over the years.

"Oh, well, I don't think that is going to happen," Rhonda said, avoiding Bea's gaze.

"What??" Bea exclaimed. "You have always said you wanted to be a mother!"

Rhonda shot her a look that said both "keep it down" and "don't forget I'm your boss" at the same time.

"Oh, sorry," Bea replied. "I guess that is none of my business. It's just that..."

Rhonda stopped her short. "I know. I don't mean to be dismissive with you, but it's just that Bill has decided—I mean, we talked about it and decided that maybe it's not such a good idea."

Bea was flabbergasted. "What do you mean 'we decided'? Rhonda, I can't believe this is how you really feel!"

Rhonda shook her head. "You know, sometimes you just have to give up things for the sake of the relationship. It's called compromise. And you know how important having Bill in my life is to me. It's just what I have to do. Now, I have a ton of work to do, so excuse me. We'll catch up later."

Bea felt a strange combination of disbelief, anger and pity. *"If that is a relationship,"* she thought, *"I'd rather do without it!"* She continued to be amazed at how a woman so competent at her job could lack so much confidence outside these walls.

Later that day, Bea made her way to the gym. It was Wednesday—her one day of exercise. Well, in truth, her one hour of exercise for the week. On Wednesdays Max had an after-school class, and Abigail went to her friend Molly's house. That left her exactly two extra hours to herself, and she relished her yoga class. She was in the locker room, changing out of her work clothes, when her friend Tamara walked in.

"Oh, hey, girl, how you doing?" Tamara asked.

"Well, you know. Hump day. Made it this far!" Bea replied.

"I hear you! I swear, if I can get through the next two days, it will be a blessing!" Tamara shook her head. "Is it Mercury Retrograde or something, because it seems everything I touch is just falling apart these days!"

"Um, not sure about that, but that sounds like my every day!" Bea said.

Tamara laughed. "You got that right! Nothing too special about that!"

Bea looked at her friend and noticed she looked more tired than usual. "Say, Tamara, maybe you just need a vacation."

"Girl, I need a LOT of vacation!" Tamara remarked. "That's just not happening!"

"Why not? You have it coming, don't you? Gosh, it seems like your last vacation was like, I don't know, two years ago?"

"Uh huh, it was. I just can't take time off. You know," she said motioning, "'needs of the business' and all that."

"I get it. But it doesn't seem fair. And besides, I think it would do you good. You look a little worn out, if you don't mind my saying."

"I am beyond worn out, but what can I do? Besides, where would I go, and who would I go with?" Tamara asked.

"I don't know, where would you like to go? How about the Bahamas—you're always talking about wanting to go there," Bea asked.

"Oh, right—me and my millions. No, I can't afford to go anywhere. You must have me confused with one of your rich friends!" Tamara shut the locker door. "And besides, who would I go with? You can't get away from those kids, and neither can anyone else I know."

"You could go by yourself. I hear they have all sorts of cruises for singles these days," Bea mentioned.

"Oh, no, not me! I could never do something like that! You just never know what those cruises are really like. And to go alone? Sitting at dinner by yourself? Uh, no thank you."

"You know, you're the second woman I've talked to today that isn't taking care of herself. What is that about?" Bea said as they grabbed their mats and headed upstairs.

"What do you mean? I'm here at this class, aren't I?" Tamara answered.

"That's not what I mean. I mean, giving yourself permission to feel good, to do what is important to you!" Bea continued, clearly frustrated.

"What has got you so all up in it?" Tamara asked.

"Oh, sorry. I didn't mean to have such an attitude! I'm just thinking about a conversation I had with a woman I know who is taking the time to do what makes her happy—and it really seems to make a difference! And I hate seeing friends unhappy," Bea added.

"Well, you're not looking all that Dana-like yourself these days," Tamara retorted.

"Exactly my point! And how perfect that you brought up Dana! I've been talking to...well, that doesn't matter, but the point is that I'm so curious as to how Dana is so, well, 'Dana-like!' And I'm noticing that there are women who are like her—like this friend I was just talking about. I'm on a 'mission' to figure it out," Bea explained.

"Well, you go, girl! You see, there you go again. The difference between you and me is that you have this idea in your head and you just go for it. I could never do that! Good for you!" Tamara looked her admiringly.

Bea looked at her friend. Tamara was a strong woman who had overcome so many odds in her life. It was amazing to her that Tamara didn't believe she could do something that simple. "Oh, I think you could, Tamara," she countered.

"Oh, no. We just have two different personalities!" Tamara said as they walked in the class. "I want to be like YOU when I grow up!" she added.

Bea laughed and mentally noted to add this to her journal that evening.

As she went to turn out the light, Bea stopped short. "Oh, shoot! I forgot to write in my journal! I'd better do it now or I'll never remember," she said to herself. She added her thoughts about her conversations that day with Rhonda and Tamara:

Things I've learned from other women:

Kelly White: Be self-aware. Do what makes you happy.

Rhonda Burton: Don't lose yourself in any relationship.

Tamara Humphrey: Stop saying you can't do something—you never know until you try!

AWARENESS

Self-awareness: Take a look at what makes you happy

Be aware of what you are giving up or what you are not even attempting to try

ACCEPTANCE

ABUNDANCE

CHAPTER 6:
FINDING YOUR VALUES

With her ever-present coffee in hand, Bea made her way up to the stage to give her notes to the production crew. It was run-through day, the day before a workshop where the speaker and technical crew do a dry-run to make sure everything goes well the next day. The speaker, Noisha Clark, was a regular client of theirs, so these days tended to be less stressful than other run-throughs. Besides, Noisha, who ran her own very successful tech company, was one of those consummate professionals who brought a positive energy to each event. Bea spied her, sitting in a rare moment alone, and decided to take advantage of the situation.

"Hey Noisha, how are we doing?" Bea asked.

"Well, hello, Bea!" Noisha answered with a smile. "Are you kidding? You guys are the best. I never worry about these events any longer!"

Bea smiled. "Good to hear. Actually, I don't get the impression you worry about too many things—you just seem like things roll off your back."

"Well, thank you for saying that, Bea." Noisha motioned for Bea to sit down. "You know, that is actually true. Not that it was always that way! But I'm truly grateful to be able to take things as they come, hang on to the important stuff, and let the others go. Makes for a much more serene life!"

Bea shook her head. "I get that! Sure wish I could be like you! You said it wasn't always like that for you? That is hard to believe! What changed?"

Noisha smiled. "It was probably about 10 years ago. I was working my way up the corporate ladder in a very well-known company. By the time I was 30, I was a Vice President, making more money than I had ever imagined and was tagged for big things in the company. I was also newly married and wanting to start a family. And for the first time in my life, I was starting to feel anxiety. It was coming out sideways: I would be rather cranky with my very patient husband. I put on 10 pounds. And I found myself getting sick all the time. But I fought through, being the good corporate citizen, until I ended up in the hospital with pneumonia. I believe it was the only way the Universe could get me to slow down! During that time when I had nothing to do but think, I really took stock of my life. On paper, it all looked fantastic: great job with a good company, making lots of money, wonderful husband, living the dream! So why was I so miserable? Then I decided to look at my life a different way. I wrote down my values. Have you ever done that, Bea?"

Bea was startled. "Ah, no. I never really thought about it!"

"Well, me either—up until that point. Like I said, I think it was the Universe's way of getting me to really look at what mattered. So I wrote down those values and then compared them to what I was doing. And do you know what I found?" Noisha asked.

"Not a match?" Bea answered with a shrug.

"Exactly! Well, there were some matches, like my family and the type of work I was doing. But those things that were most important to me—family, integrity, creativity—were not getting much airtime. I decided it was time to make some changes. And that is how my company came to be. I made a conscious decision from that day forward to only concern myself with that which is right FOR ME and to release the rest. And, so far, so good."

"I'd say so!" Bea answered. "Very impressive! You know, you always have such a positive vibe whenever I see you. It's nice to know how and why you got to that place! Thanks so much for sharing your story!"

Noisha smiled. "It's my pleasure, my dear. Now, shall we get back to work? I think we've got a show to do!"

That night, Bea reflected on how much Kelly White's story overlapped with Noisha's. There seemed to be something very positive in all this self-reflection and the process of slowing down to see it. She added to her journal an entry about her conversation with Noisha.

Things I've learned from other women:

Kelly White: Be self-aware. Do what makes you happy.

Rhonda Burton: Don't lose yourself in any relationship.

Tamara Humphrey: Stop saying you can't do something—you never know until you try!

Noisha Clark: Focus on your values.

AWARENESS

Self-awareness: take a look at what makes you happy.

Be aware of what you are giving up or what you are not even attempting to try.

Values: write them down!

ACCEPTANCE

ABUNDANCE

CHAPTER 7:
WHOSE LIFE ARE YOU LIVING?

Bea was lost in thought, busily scanning her emails to see which urgent message needed her attention next. Waiting for her kids to be let out of school was just one more chance she had to sneak in a little more work. She glanced at her watch: They were getting out a little late again. She lifted up a silent thanks for whatever it was that was keeping them tied up a bit longer. It gave her a minute more to finish another reply. As she started composing her note, she was jostled back to reality by the appearance of a woman half running across the playground. It was Sheila, late again.

"Oh, my goodness, I can't believe I made it here on time today!" she exhaled, pausing now to catch her breath. "You would NOT believe that traffic today! I really should have left the office earlier, but, you know how it is—someone always is asking you to do something right when you have to leave!"

"Yes, I'm familiar with that!" Bea agreed. "That's why I take the train—can't argue with the train schedules!"

"Really?" Sheila asked. "Can you really tell someone you have to leave? Oh, I could never do that! I'd just feel so guilty! I don't want them thinking that I'm a slacker or something. Hmmm...maybe I SHOULD think about taking the train. Do you think that's a good idea?"

Bea shrugged. "I don't know—it works for me. Say, what are you sending in with Brendan for the back-to-school-night treats? I was thinking of running to the store and picking up some cookies. Do you want me to grab you something?"

"Oh, I am making cupcakes tonight. Not sure how we're going to fit that in, but..." Sheila trailed off as the school doors opened, releasing the exuberant children.

"Really? You're making something? Why not buy it?" Bea asked, as she bent down to hug her son. He gave her a quick hug and asked, "Can you hold my backpack? Sam and I are just going to play over there for a minute!" and he was off. "Just for a minute," she shouted back to him, as he hurriedly waved goodbye.

"Honestly," she said, turning back to Sheila. "Why I bother rushing here to get him... Anyway, the cupcakes?"

Sheila was deep in conversation with her daughter. "I know, sweetie, but you know you have piano lessons in an hour," she was saying to a little girl who obviously had ideas of her own. "I hear you that you want to play and I understand that this is important to you. OK, just for one minute, though." She turned back to Bea, shaking her head. "I read that it is important to validate your children's feelings, you know. Lord knows I don't need one more thing to add to the list of mothering things I'm doing wrong! Oh, and I know what you mean about this pickup routine! But I heard on an NPR interview while I was driving in that it's important for the children to know you are there for them. I just hate it when traffic messes me up! Can't imagine what it's doing to my kid when she doesn't see me after school right away!"

Bea just stared and said, "Um, I don't think that's what they meant...", but Sheila continued, "Now, what were you saying? Oh, right, the cupcakes. Oh, thanks, but I could never send in store-bought! I overheard MaryLou talking about a time when Gloria sent in cookies, and I just could not bear to be talked about like that! But don't let that stop you! You know, you're just so much stronger than I am! Now, where is that girl? We have piano lessons, then her brother's game, then homework, and THEN I have to take a conference call. How am I going to fit dinner in there? I guess we are having takeout again. I feel so guilty about that—second time this week! The kids really should be eating more healthy foods. Well, I better run—have a great evening!"

Bea just shook her head. "You, too. Good luck with everything. And let me know if you change your mind and want me to pick you up something at the store. Sounds like you have your hands full!"

"Oh, gosh, the cupcakes! When am I going to fit that in?!" Sheila exclaimed as she walked away. "Well, guess sleep is not in the picture for me tonight! See you tomorrow!"

Bea saw Sheila walk over to negotiate with her daughter. Bea couldn't help but just shake her head again as she turned to find her son.

That night Bea made another entry in her journal:

Things I've learned from other women:

Kelly White: Be self-aware. Do what makes you happy.

Rhonda Burton: Don't lose yourself in any relationship.

Tamara Humphrey: Stop saying you can't do something—you never know until you try!

Noisha Clark: Focus on your values.

Sheila Cummings: Do not become overly reliant upon the opinions of others, living your life according to what "they" say.

I can't imagine Dana Meadows worrying about those kinds of things, Bea thought. *Maybe that's part of the answer.*

And with that, she drifted off to sleep, ready for the next day.

CHAPTER 8:
THE PROJECT—PHASE 2

Friday lunchtime—and that meant her weekly trip to Velma. Bea hadn't talked to her since she started her new "project" and knew she'd get Velma's take on it, whether she wanted it or not!

It didn't take long before Velma brought it up herself. "So, did you find the secret to the 'Dana Meadows life' yet?" she asked.

"Funny you should ask..." Bea started.

"No! You did?! Don't tell me you finally met Dana! Honey, you have GOT it! Tell Velma all about it!" Velma gushed.

Bea shook her head and laughed. "No, no, no... nothing quite as exciting as that!" she said. "No, but you did inspire me to do a little research project. So, I've been taking your advice and talking with other women. And it's been pretty interesting so far."

"Do tell!" Velma said.

"Well, so far I talked with women I see, you know, in my 'normal' life—other moms on the playground or at sporting events—and one woman who is a client. There are a couple who I think have 'it' and a couple who have something else that, um, I don't think I want. Some good info so far, but I think I have a ways to go before discovering the holy Dana Meadows grail!"

"Well, it sounds like you got yourself started on that Awareness journey! So, what is that 'it' you're talking about?" Velma asked.

"Well, it's hard to say...you know, like that 'magic' you said Dana has," Bea replied.

"Uh, huh. Don't you know that! Well, how's this for an idea—and I might just be spitting in the wind—but what if you made a list of what it is that Dana has, besides money? And then find some ladies that have that, too. Then you could talk to them!" Velma smiled proudly.

"Well, Velma, you may be on to something! What a great idea! How did you get so smart?" Bea said.

"Well, I have a trick or two up my sleeve," Velma answered. "You just caught me on a good day! Say, do you know Ling Wu? She's one of my regulars. Lord, that woman has it all—and sweet, too! Mmm, mmm, mmm..." she said, shaking her head. "You should talk to her!"

"I think I do know her," said Bea. "I think her daughter takes ballet with mine. Great suggestion, Velma! I'll add her to my list!"

"Keep going—you're doing great things here! And when you're done, who knows what other women you're going to help along the way! You're just making Velma so proud!" she said with a smile.

"Well, stay tuned," said Bea. "You just never know!"

Later that night, Bea thought about what Velma had said and decided to make a list of the women she wanted to talk to. She thought about her concept of the Queen Bee: Who fit those criteria? She reviewed her initial thoughts on what she called a "Queen Bee," or what Velma would call "the Dana Meadows life":

Qualities of a Queen Bee:

comfortable in own skin

positive energy

not concerned about what others think

doing amazing things

confident

successful

So who did she know who fit that bill? Well, there was Ling Wu, the one Velma suggested. Then there was Madeline Fox, a woman who had overcome amazing difficulties and always seemed to have a smile on her face. Peggy DeBaar also came to mind, as she had that "it" quality. And lastly, a woman from her church, Miriam Mavens, who was practically a lesson in gratitude herself. Yes, these women would definitely give her answers!

CHAPTER 9:
FORGIVENESS

As luck would have it, the first person Bea ran into Monday morning was her colleague, Madeline Fox. As expected, Madeline greeted Bea with a warm smile. "Don't you look pretty today!" she said.

Bea couldn't help but smile back. "Well, thank you, Madeline! That certainly starts my week off right!"

"Oh, so glad!" Madeline answered back.

"Say," Bea added, "I was thinking about you over the weekend and have a couple of questions I'd love to ask you for a project I'm doing. Would you be free for lunch today?"

"Me? Wow, I'm flattered! Sure! I have the account review at 11 but can meet you in the break room after that, if that works for you."

"Perfect! See you then!"

"So, you were thinking about me over the weekend?" Madeline asked Bea as they sat down to lunch.

"Yes...well, let's say you came to mind. I'm on a 'quest' of sorts to figure out how to be like Dana Meadows," Bea explained.

Madeline laughed. "Oh, let me know when you figure that out! But seriously, why did you think of me?"

"Well, I was thinking of women who are like Dana, in that they are comfortable in their own skin, they have great positive energy, they're not concerned about what others think, they're confident, successful, and are doing amazing things. As I said, you came to mind."

"Wow, how flattering! Just to be thought of in the same category as Dana—guess I have you fooled!" Madeline said with a wink.

Bea smiled. "Me and a lot of other people!"

"Well, thank you," Madeline continued. "I truly am flattered. And yes, I guess, without sounding a bit full of myself, I am proud to feel very comfortable in my own skin. And I think that actually enables the rest to flow. What do you think?"

"It seems to make a lot of sense to me. But, what I was curious about with you is, how did you get that way? I know you've had some challenges in your life."

A shy smile crossed Madeline's lips. "It is true; mine has not been the life most would have chosen. Did you want to hear my story? How much time do you have?"

Bea nodded. "Yes, I would love hearing it! I'm good for a while if you are!"

"OK, I have a few minutes," Madeline continued. "Let's see...where to begin. Well, I guess maybe I'll just start when I was about five. I lived in a rural part of Vietnam in a beautiful farming community. I had a lovely family and a happy childhood—up until that point. And then one day the bombing started. I don't have a lot of memories from that other than confusion and terror. My mother hid me in a rice paddy—and that was the last I saw of her. I was left there all alone, very scared and very hungry, until a U.S. soldier found me and brought me to his camp. I was then transported to an orphanage, where I stayed for three years. It was a stark contrast to my rich beginning, and I really retreated inwardly and became very ill. The orphanage transferred me to hospital in Germany, where I stayed until I was strong enough to be placed into adoption. By this time I was 11 years old, not the age most people are looking for. I was on the verge of giving up hope, once more, when I was blessed to have angels rescue me from that horrible situation. My adoptive family brought me to this country and showed me that life was good, that people could be trusted, and that I was worth saving. It's truly a miracle."

Bea shook her head. She'd heard parts of the story before and could never quite figure out how this lovely woman could have come from such a horrific start. "I would have to agree with you on the miracle point, Madeline. But don't you feel angry sometimes? How can you always walk around with a smile on your face?"

In true form, Madeline smiled. "Oh, trust me, there has been a lifetime of anger in me! You didn't know me 'then,' when I was a horribly angry teenager. I did a lot of acting out—and a lot of abusive behavior, mainly to myself. I just didn't feel worthy of anything."

"So what caused the change?" Bea asked.

"One word," Madeline answered. "Forgiveness. Oh, that came from many years of therapy, and many years of my dear adoptive parents struggling to help me believe in their love. I had to learn to forgive those who had inflicted pain on me, those I judged as evil, and those who I had every right to hate. But most of all, I had to forgive myself. I had to forgive myself for judging myself as anything other than the perfect being that I am. That was the hardest! Self-acceptance—such a hard thing, and the key to it all."

"You really are an inspiration, Madeline," Bea said, tears forming in her eyes. "I don't know if I could have done it."

"It's interesting—I didn't think I could, either. But, I am so very, very grateful that I decided to choose life. That I decided to choose love. That I decided that I was worth it. It really all comes down to choice. Are you willing to choose to believe in yourself or not? Are you willing to choose to forgive yourself and others, or not? Are you willing to live a full life, or not? I think you can tell where my choices lay."

"Absolutely! And so, having made this choice, did everything fall in place for you?" Bea asked.

"It's a work in process. We all are. We are faced with choices every day—some bigger than others. But I stayed steadfast in my desires, I let others love me until I could love myself, and now I am grateful to be able to pass some of that love back on. That's why I do all the charity work I do."

"Well, I for one am very grateful for you! And yes, you do deserve to be mentioned in the same breath as Dana Meadows!" Bea exclaimed.

"I'm honored," Madeline said, eyes casting downward and hand on heart. She looked up and met Bea's gaze. "Passing it on—it's what we need to do!"

"Indeed," Bea answered. "Indeed we do."

That night, with Madeline's story still ringing in her head, Bea opened her journal and made the following entry:

Things I've learned from other women:

Kelly White: Be self-aware. Do what makes you happy.

Rhonda Burton: Don't lose yourself in any relationship.

Tamara Humphrey: Stop saying you can't do something—you never know until you try!

Noisha Clark: Focus on your values.

Sheila Cummings: Do not become overly reliant upon the opinions of others, living your life according to what "they" say.

Madeline Fox: Forgiveness—of self and others. Life is all about choices.

AWARENESS

Self-awareness: take a look at what makes you happy.

Be aware of what you are giving up or what you are not even attempting to try.

Values: write them down!

Be aware of your choices.

ACCEPTANCE

Forgive the judgments you hold on yourself and others.

ABUNDANCE

CHAPTER 10:
LETTING GO OF THE SHOULDS

"Sweetie, what is the name of the girl in your ballet class—you know, the one we gave a ride home to once?" Bea asked her daughter as they drove to her lessons.

"Um, Ashley? Why?" Abigail answered.

"Oh, right! Someone suggested I talk to her mom, and I couldn't remember what her name was. I didn't want to say the wrong name when I met her!" Bea answered.

"Yeah, that would be lame," Abigail noted, as they pulled into the parking lot. Bea turned off the car and started to unbuckle her seatbelt.

"What are you doing? You're not going in with me, are you? I think I'm old enough to walk to my lessons, Mother."

"Calm down, Miss," Bea said. "I've got a couple of errands to run, if you don't mind. I'll meet you back here when you're done."

"OK...see ya!" Abby answered, visibly relieved.

Bea was shaking her head, lost in the wonderment of how her daughter was changing, when she was brought quickly back to reality by a car pulling in next to her. As she swerved to walk around it, the driver rolled down her window and said, "Sorry about that!" It was Ling Wu.

"Oh, no worries—I was lost in thought and didn't notice you!" Bea answered, as Ling's daughter scrambled out of the car, and with a quick goodbye to her mother, dashed to catch up with Abigail.

Ling shook her head. "Kids!" she said with a smile, getting out of her car.

"That's what I was thinking about when I nearly walked into you! When did my little girl, who yesterday didn't want to leave my side, start to find me so....embarrassing?" Bea said.

"Probably about the same age you thought that of your mother!" Ling answered. "As they say, it's 'age-appropriate behavior!' It's all good!"

"You're so right!" Bea said. "It's Ling, right? I'm Abigail's mom, Bea. I think we met a while back," Bea said, extending her hand.

Ling shook it warmly. "Oh right! You're the one Velma told me to talk to!"

Bea laughed. "That Velma—she's a character! I think she thinks she's my agent! But yes, I would love to grab a coffee and chat. Do you have time now?"

"Actually, I do!" Ling said. "I was just going to sit here and do emails until Ashley came back, but that sounds like a better proposition! Let's do it!"

Bea and Ling walked to the local diner and settled in a booth in the back. After a few minutes of getting reacquainted, Bea asked, "So, I'm curious what Velma said to you about me."

Ling said, "Well, she said something about you doing a research project, and that I was the perfect person to talk to. Not a lot of details. But you know Velma—she can be very convincing!"

Bea laughed. "Well, she wouldn't let it go, that's for sure! Yes, I am doing a project, of sorts—for myself. I work for a company that produces events, and we did the Dana Meadows conference not long ago."

"Oh, I love Dana! I had thought about going to that but couldn't take the time off. I did hear good things about it, though," Ling mentioned.

"Thanks— it is always great when we can produce events featuring such quality women like her!" Bea answered. "Well, getting back to my project: An interesting thing happened at that event that really had me puzzled. I noticed that the women who came in seemed so confident and self-possessed, and I wondered why they would need to go to an empowerment workshop. But then, as the session started, I noticed that these same women seemed to change, to become more insecure—like they just gave their power away. It made me start to wonder two things: first, why do women do that, and second, is it really possible to be so secure in yourself, like a Dana Meadows? Well, I guess three questions— the third being, if so, how do you get and stay there? Here's where Velma comes in. I was telling her this, and she suggested I start talking to women to find out what they think. And, she suggested I talk to you, as a woman who seems to have 'it.' So tell me, Ling, how do you do it? How do you seem so self-possessed and comfortable in your own skin?"

"Whew!" Ling answered. "You're comparing me to Dana Meadows? I'm so flattered! And that sounds like an excellent project—I'd love to hear your findings! But, you ask how I do it? Probably the same way Dana and millions of others do it: one day at a time. Maybe it would help to tell you my story?"

"Oh, please do!" Bea said excitedly. "If you want to, that is."

Ling smiled. "With pleasure! All in the name of research!" And she began her narrative.

"I was born in California to parents who had recently emigrated to the U.S. from China. While they assimilated well into this country, the traditions of the homeland were revered. My father, as you would imagine, was the patriarch of the family. He was the breadwinner in the family and, as you might also imagine, set the rules. However, in reality, my mother was really the stronger of the two and was a force to be reckoned with. She had opinions on everything, and as a result, I learned early that it was easier to go with the flow rather than swim upstream. So her opinions and thoughts became my opinions and thoughts. I was the good girl, doing what was expected of me. Or should I say, always striving to exceed expectations.

"This living according to what others wanted or expected spilled over into every corner of my life. As I got older and interested in boys, well, you can imagine that I became rather chameleon-like in their presence. Whatever they liked, I liked. You're a jock? Well, I love sports. You're more interested in string theory? I became a science geek. And on and on.

"When it came time for me to go to college, I can't remember ever having any say in what I was going to do. But, on the other hand, I really didn't give it much thought. My parents expected that I would be an engineer, so that's what I did. And, of course, I couldn't live far from home, so I went to UC Berkeley—and commuted.

"All was 'fine'—a family favorite word—until I actually started at Berkeley. Here I thought I was picking the 'safe' school, when I actually was at the epicenter of individual thought! It was so hard for me initially in classes where the professors and fellow classmates actually wanted to hear my opinions! I was stopped in my tracks. What did I think? Or more appropriately, what did my mother think? It was really difficult to learn to find my voice. But gradually I did—not that my parents were all that thrilled with it! You think our daughters are bad? Try going from a totally controlled environment to that of an individual thinker! Whew—there were some heady moments!"

Ling smiled at the thought, sipped her coffee, and continued.

"Well, we all lived through that, and I graduated— Cum Laude, of course, as was expected—with my degree in Electrical Engineering. I had little interest in the profession. But that drive to please, to do what I should do, was very strong still, so I got a job with a big tech company. Great company, great job. Everyone was very proud of me. Check that one off the list.

"Then there was the next thing: marriage. I wasn't getting any younger, and rather than face a possible arrangement, I grabbed the first guy who came by who said he loved me. I was married at 25 and had my first son at 28. I worked for a while and of course tried to do it all—you know, the Superwoman role?"

Bea laughed. "Yes, I'm more than a little familiar with it!"

Ling continued, "Well, I don't know about you, but that is an unsustainable model! Something had to go—and it was looking like it was either my sanity or my marriage. In one of my first moves of stepping out of my comfort zone, I listened to myself instead of others and did what was right for me. My husband and I split. It was one of the hardest—and best—things I ever did.

"But being a single mom was not easy by a long shot. Trying to juggle it all and not be overwhelmed by the guilt when I couldn't nearly did me in. But I persevered. Meanwhile, I started talking yoga classes... which led me to other 'enlightenment' courses... and I started to find the real 'me.' It was quite an internal journey!

"And it had an impact externally as well. I finally faced the fact that while I was really good at my job, I had no passion for it! Fortunately, I worked for a big company that had a lot of room to move... and I eventually found my way into the technical writing group. This really helped me find my passion for writing—far more than creating electrical components! And interestingly, the more I became aligned with who I really was, the happier I became, and the better my relationships became as well. My estranged husband and I started seeing each other again, and found that when we let go of the way we felt we SHOULD be, we actually liked the 'real' version of each other. We've now been married for 20 years, with a few off for good behavior!"

Bea laughed. "That is an amazing story! I am in awe of how you were able to transform!"

Ling smiled, "Well, it wasn't always easy, but it was so worth it. Letting go of the 'shoulds' and coming back to me made all the difference in the world. I'm a better person, a better partner, and a better mom. And, when the time came for us to move here, it made it that much easier for me to negotiate for my job. I knew what worked for me and my family and what didn't, I knew what I had to offer, and I knew where my passions laid. Now I'm the managing editor of a tech publication and couldn't be happier. I consider myself a continuing work in progress—a person who lives a 'should-free' life!"

Bea smiled. "I love it. I am so grateful to Velma for recommending I talk to you! This has been great! Thanks so much!"

"My pleasure indeed," Ling answered. "Now, I think we'd best get back to our cars before our girls get there!"

Bea could not stop thinking about Ling's inspiring story. That night, when she pulled out her journal, it was easy to remember the lesson to record:

Things I've learned from other women:

Kelly White: Be self-aware. Do what makes you happy.

Rhonda Burton: Don't lose yourself in any relationship.

Tamara Humphrey: Stop saying you can't do something—you never know until you try!

Noisha Clark: Focus on your values.

Sheila Cummings: Do not become overly reliant upon the opinions of others, living your life according to what "they" say.

Madeline Fox: Forgiveness—of self and others.

Life is all about choices.

Ling Wu: Let go of the shoulds!

AWARENESS

Self-awareness: take a look at what makes you happy.

Be aware of what you are giving up or what you are not even attempting to try.

Values: write them down!

Be aware of your choices.

Do something because it is right for you, not just because someone or something told you that you should do it.

ACCEPTANCE

Forgive the judgments you hold on yourself and others.

ABUNDANCE

CHAPTER 11:
FINDING YOUR FOCUS

Bea checked herself in the bathroom mirror one last time and took a deep breath. "I can do this," she said to herself, as she walked down the hall to her lunch meeting. Her company had long held a policy of encouraging employees to hold an "open door" meeting with upper management, but Bea had never felt the need—or the desire—to do so. But this year, when the annual policy reminder arrived in her inbox, Bea decided to go for it. She had arranged a working lunch with Peggy DeBaar, the Senior Vice President of Productions and her third-level manager. While she and Peggy knew each other enough to exchange pleasantries, this would be the first time she had an actual conversation with her. Bea reached the well-appointed office a few minutes ahead of the scheduled time and was directed to have a seat while Peggy's assistant got her a coffee. Bea could feel her heart pounding as she wiped her hands on her skirt to try to dry them. She did not want her first impression to be that of sweaty palms!

As she sat and sipped her coffee, Bea took in the surroundings. Everything here gave the impression of someone who had "made it": the comfortable furniture, the artwork on the walls, the calm atmosphere. So different from her space a few floors below. She allowed herself to dream for a moment, of having a corner office with a view and an assistant to take care of the details. *Hmmm, I could get used to that,* she thought. As she was settling into her daydream, the office door opened, and a woman in a tailored suit emerged, smiling and walking towards Bea with her hand extended.

"Bea, I'm so sorry to keep you waiting!" Peggy exclaimed, as she shook Bea's hand with both of hers. "Please, come in!"

They walked into the office, and Peggy ushered her to a small conference table, already set for lunch. "I hope you don't mind that I took the liberty of ordering us some salads," Peggy said.

"Works for me!" Bea answered with a smile as she took her seat.

After a few minutes of conversation on the unusually warm weather they'd been having, and a review of what each was doing over the holidays, Peggy moved seamlessly into the business at hand.

"You know, my life here is one big meeting, but I can't tell you how pleased I was to get the meeting notice on this lunch! We're really serious about this open-door policy, and I could probably count on one hand how many times people have taken us up on it. It is such a delight to be able to spend one-on-one time with you. How can I help you today?" she asked.

Bea smiled. "Yes, well, it's the first time I've ever, um, felt the desire to take you up on the offer. It's not that I didn't appreciate the opportunity in the past—I just didn't have anything to talk about. Or I didn't think I did," she added.

"So what's different this year?" Peggy asked.

"Well, I guess I am," Bea answered. "It started a few months ago at the Dana Meadows event. It was a combination of things: First, there's Dana herself. I've always been in awe of her and, well, wanted to be like her when I grew up!"

Peggy laughed. "Don't we all!"

Bea smiled. "And then there were the women who attended the event. They all seemed so confident and powerful when they arrived, and I couldn't figure out why they were there. And then, during the event, it seemed to change. It was like they forgot who they were when they sat down and became, I don't know, 'less than.' I don't know if that makes sense..."

"I know exactly what you mean," Peggy noted with a nod. "I've seen the same things happen over and over again—and not just at those events. It happens here every day! Trust me—it happens when women come up here to the executive floor! I see strong, capable women who become somebody else when they step off that elevator. It really is uncanny. It's a great observation, Bea."

Bea smiled and relaxed, enjoying the recognition. It gave her the confidence she needed to continue. "So, all of this got me to wondering: How does she do it? How does Dana stay so 'powerful'? I really wanted to know. So I was talking with my... uh, friend, and she suggested that I do a little project and talk to other women and get their opinions. And that's when I thought of coming here and asking you."

"Great question!" Peggy sat back and smiled. "I'm not sure I have the answer, but I can give you my opinion for sure. I don't really know Dana, although we have met several times. And yes, she is the same confident person you see on stage when she is off stage. She exudes confidence. It's very contagious, and it makes you want more! I get that! My opinion is that she is a woman who is comfortable in her own skin. She seems to have done a lot of inner work and knows who she is—and is not afraid to put it out there. It is a great lesson for us all."

"Well, I think you do the same," Bea noted.

Peggy smiled. "Well, thank you for saying that, Bea. That is very kind of you. I hope I do. I work on it. It's not always easy, but it sure beats trying to be something you're not!"

"So, here is my question to you," Bea asked, now fully warmed up. "How do you do it? I mean, how did you get to this place—personally and professionally? What's your secret?"

"Two things," Peggy answered. "Focus and mentors. I am not sure which is the harder to find these days! But for me, I couldn't find the mentors until I knew my focus. I had to really take the time to figure out what was important to me: What were 'nice to haves,' and what were 'deal breakers'? That applied in all aspects of my life. I had to learn to believe in myself, that I was worthy of dreaming big. And then, once I did that, I was ready to go. Why not shoot for the corner office? You know, I started off like you, in the event-planning office. But I knew I had more to offer and decided to find a way to get to the top.

"The first thing I did was to look for other people who had 'made it' and ask them how they did it. Just like you are today," Peggy noted with a smile. "There were only two women in the executive ranks back then, and I made a point of getting to know them. And I got to know the men as well. I wanted to see the similarities and the differences and figure out what worked for me. One of the women took me under her wing and became a mentor to me—someone who I could go to for advice and counsel. And one of the men became a sponsor—someone who believed in me and helped to promote me internally. It's important to have both, I discovered," she added.

"Great advice!" Bea agreed. "I can see why that would make a difference. So focus and mentors were what helped you..."

Peggy jumped in. "Actually, there is one other thing I just thought about. Languaging. It's something I have really come to notice lately, and it's become my personal mission to change this in this company. Let me explain.

"When I was working my way up the corporate ladder here, I started attending more and more meetings where there would be senior executives in attendance. I knew it would be a great opportunity for them to get to know me, so I made it a point to say something at each meeting. Sometimes I had some really great ideas that I'd put out there, and then someone else would echo what I just said and get the credit for the idea! It was infuriating! I was expressing this to my mentor one day, and she pointed out a very crucial thing: It wasn't what I was saying, it was HOW I was saying it. I had a tendency to start off with 'I think' or 'I was just thinking' or 'I was wondering.' These are all phrases that dilute your message. It puts you in a 'less than' position. Once this was brought to my attention, I noticed I did it a lot! It was a very unconscious way of 'easing in' to the conversation. It still gave me an 'out,' because I, again, unconsciously, had a greater need to be accepted and liked than to be respected and heard. When I used that kind of language, people would nod politely and smile, which I took as a good thing... but someone else would swoop in with more confidence, and they would be HEARD. I have since taken to bringing this to the attention of younger women in the firm. I think it's a societal issue, similar to what you observed about those women at the Dana Meadows event. It is us giving away our power, without even realizing it! We are powerful beings, and it's time we realized it and embraced it."

Peggy sat back and smiled. "OK, enough of my soapbox! Can you tell I am passionate about this?"

Bea laughed. "I think—I mean, I KNOW you are! This is really great information for me. I so appreciate it!"

"Ah, indeed, my pleasure! And now, it's time for me to get back to one of those meetings! This has been a breath of fresh air for me, Bea! Thank you so much for coming in!"

"Well, thank you!" Bea answered, shaking her hand. "I'll let others know that it's not so scary at the top!"

"Please do...and come back again," Peggy added, as Bea headed back to work.

That evening, Bea couldn't wait to add Peggy's wisdom to her journal. She wrote:

Things I've learned from other women:
Kelly White: Be self-aware. Do what makes you happy.
Rhonda Burton: Don't lose yourself in any relationship.
Tamara Humphrey: Stop saying you can't do

something—you never know until you try!

Noisha Clark: Focus on your values.

Sheila Cummings: Do not become overly reliant upon the opinions of others, living your life according to what "they" say.

Madeline Fox: Forgiveness—of self and others. Life is all about choices.

Ling Wu: Let go of the shoulds!

Peggy DeBaar: Find your focus. Get mentors and sponsors. Watch your languaging!

AWARENESS

Self-awareness: take a look at what makes you happy.

Be aware of what you are giving up or what you are not even attempting to try.

Values: write them down!

Be aware of your choices.

Do something because it is right for you, not just because someone or something told you that you should do it.

Watch not only what you say, but how you say it.

ACCEPTANCE

Forgive the judgments you hold on yourself and others.

Find your focus, and stick to it.

ABUNDANCE

Accept the wisdom of others.

CHAPTER 12:
AN ATTITUDE OF GRATITUDE

"Moooommmmmmm! Hurry up! We're going to be late!" Abigail yelled up the stairs.

"Again...." Bea mumbled under her breath, as she rummaged through her jewelry box looking for her earrings. "I'm coming!" she answered. "Is your brother ready?"

Abby looked over at her brother, engrossed in a video game. "He will be," she yelled back. Abby walked over and turned off the TV.

"Hey! Not fair—I was about to get to Level 2!" Max exclaimed.

"Let's GO," Abby pleaded, ignoring his reaction. "I don't want to be late again!"

A minute later the family was on their way to church. "A minor miracle," Bea mused. She was pleased with the way her daughter had taken to her confirmation class, although she had a sneaking suspicion it had more to do with a certain boy who was also in the class. *Whatever it takes,* she thought.

The kids were off to their Sunday school classes, and Bea made her way to the church kitchen to find Miriam. Miriam Mavens had been heading up the "coffee hour" committee for about as long as Bea could remember. She was a perpetually cheerful woman who seemed to love serving the congregation their cookies and coffee after the service each week. Bea found her busy at the sink.

"Hi, Miriam," Bea said, "I'm here to help you!"

"Well, hello, sweetheart! I saw you were on the list today, and it just brightened my day!" Miriam said with a smile.

"Oh, you're just trying to butter me up so I'll do this more often," Bea joked.

"Is it working?" Miriam asked.

"Not yet. Keep going," Bea answered with a grin. "So, how can I help you?"

"Be a dear and grab those cookies over there and arrange them on the plates, would you? Thanks, Bea!" Miriam said as she carried a platter out to the table.

Bea watched Miriam throughout the coffee hour, captivated by her ability to stay cheerful and upbeat with even the grouchiest parishioner. And it wasn't an act—she seemed genuinely happy to be of service. She made a mental note to ask her about it later.

It was while washing dishes that Bea finally got her chance. "Say, Miriam," she began. "I'm curious, how long have you actually been doing this job?"

"What job is that, honey?" Miriam asked, putting the platter in the cupboard.

"Coffee hour," Bea answered.

"Oh!" Miriam laughed. "Sorry—I just never think of it as a job! I guess I'm going on 10 years now! It's just part of what I do!"

Bea shook her head. "You're a better woman than I!" she said.

"Well, I don't know about that," Miriam answered. "Look at all you do! You're raising those two beautiful children by yourself, you have that great job, and here you are helping me out! I think you're pretty darn good yourself!"

"Well, thank you!" Bea responded. "So, I was watching you during the coffee hour, and you look like you really enjoy it. Even after all this time."

"Oh, I do!" Miriam agreed. "I am just so grateful to be able to serve in this way. And to be able to see my friends, to meet new members, and to greet guests— well, it's almost like I am hosting a party every week!"

"I guess when you put it that way, it makes it a lot more fun!" Bea said. She paused, thinking of other women who made their work seem like fun. Of course, Dana came to mind. Bea decided to ask Miriam her opinion.

"Here's another question for you. You know who Dana Meadows is, right?" Bea asked.

"Well, of course!" Miriam noted.

"Well, I have been doing this 'research project,' asking a lot of women what they think, and I'd be curious about your opinion. How do you think she does it? You know, how she seems to be someone who has it all together, that is?" Bea asked.

"What an interesting project—and question," Miriam said. "Yes, she does seem to be a woman who is comfortable in her own skin, doesn't she? I can't be sure, but I think it comes from knowing herself and doing what aligns with her purpose. Like I said, I can't speak for her, but that's what works for me."

"I'm so glad you said that," Bea answered. "You have always struck me as someone who is very self-assured and always so positive. It's nice to hear your 'secret!' So how did you figure out your purpose?"

Miriam laughed. "Oh, that's a long story!" she said.

"That's OK," Bea replied. "I have to wait around until Abby gets out of class, so I have the time, if you do."

"OK, well, if you're really interested. Let's finish up these dishes and have a seat. I think there's a cup or two of coffee left in the pot."

With coffee in hand, Bea grabbed a seat to listen to Miriam's story.

"Well, let's see—where to start? OK, well, as you can probably imagine, I have always been what they call a 'people pleaser,'" Miriam began with a smile. "There's a lot to be said for that, but there is a lot that is not so great about it as well. For me, I just went about my life from a very early age, trying to make sure everyone was happy with me. That meant becoming very good at figuring out what others wanted. But it also meant that I had no idea what I wanted. Everything in my life was predicated on what someone else liked, wanted, or needed. That works really well on the outside, but inside, well, you start to get lost. It seems strange now, but I really lost touch with my feelings. I had no idea how I really felt, which left me more often than not feeling confused and depressed. I remember one time my husband said something to me, and I became agitated. When he asked me what was wrong, I literally had no idea. I just knew something didn't feel right, so I did what I usually did: avoided him for the next few days until I could figure it out. Times like that would be a great excuse for me to find a way to numb myself out, to escape that uncomfortable feeling—whatever it was! I would sneak a little drink of whatever was in our cupboard at the time. This worked—for a while. And then even that wouldn't take away that uncomfortable feeling and actually started causing more bad feelings of guilt and shame. It got very ugly for a while, I'm sorry to say."

Bea was fascinated by this side of Miriam that she had never known and listened intently as she continued.

"Without getting into all of it, let's just fast forward and say I'm grateful that I sobered up! And then the real fun started! Remember me saying I had no connection to my feelings? Well, now, without anything to numb them out, they ALL came back—with a vengeance! I was a big puddle of feelings! It took a lot of time and work on my part to learn not only what they were, but to accept them! All of them! Even the ones that I would have thought of as ugly. I had to accept my human condition. I joined a 12-step program. I read a lot of self-help books, I went to a lot of seminars and retreats, and I had a great therapist. I committed to getting healthy and whole—and I believed I was worth it! Oh, not at first, mind you, but gradually I did.

"As you can also probably assume, my faith became very important to me once again. I say 'once again' because as a child I loved my church and was very involved in the youth programs—a lot like your kids. And then there was college and my 20s. I went the way of so many others; I just found other things that became more important to me. When I got sober, I began to look back at what had been important to me at other times in my life, and took the time to reassess each one. I kept coming back to this issue of faith. It was what had served me in the past, what had given my life meaning. I couldn't overlook that. I decided to find a way to explore that aspect in more detail, and that is when I found this church. I knew from the minute I sat in that pew that I was home. I had had a 'God-sized hole' inside that I had been trying to fill with everything else, but knew when I got here what the real answer was for me. And I haven't looked back."

Miriam smiled, lost in thought for a moment. "Oh, but your question was about purpose. Well, who can say for absolute certainty what their purpose is? Maybe someday when we are looking down from heaven, it will all make sense. I can only go on what I feel in my bones. And what that is for me is gratitude. I am eternally grateful for the life I have been given, and see it as a blessing that I can be here one more day. And because of that, I feel my purpose is to serve, with gratitude, and be willing to do what the Lord asks me to do. For now, it's doing things like this coffee hour, or visiting the sick and elderly. What a gift I have been given to have the opportunity to serve in this way! It just makes my heart smile!"

"Well, you certainly exude that!" Bea added. "I have always marveled at how you can always have a smile on your face! Now I know! Thank you so much for sharing your story with me!"

"Oh, thank you for listening! I'm always glad to put in my two cents' worth! And you know, thinking about your question about Dana Meadows, I think part of her secret is finding gratitude. What is it she says? Awareness, Acceptance… oh, what's the last one?" Miriam asked.

"Abundance," Bea answered.

"Right! Abundance. That is where the gratitude comes in. My grandmother always used to say to me, 'Mim'—she called me 'Mim' back then—'Mim, you can catch more flies with honey than vinegar.' Well, when I was a little girl, I was so confused by that. My grandmother lived on a farm, and I couldn't figure out why she would want to catch flies at all!" Miriam chuckled at the thought.

"But then as I got a little older, I thought she meant that you need to be nice all the time. And we know how that worked out! Well, now I have come to see it as having to do with your attitude. And when you exude an 'attitude of gratitude' as the young people say these days, then miracles just happen. I think that is true for Miss Dana Meadows as well, don't you think?"

"I think you are on to something, Miriam," Bea agreed. "Thank you so much for your time and your wisdom! It has really helped me!"

"Oh, please!" Miriam waved her off with a smile. "Just grateful to have the chance to sit and chat! Now, you'd better go gather up those kids before they start wondering what happened to you!"

"You think they'd notice?" Bea smiled. "Well, they will when they get hungry. I'd best be going. Thanks again—and see you next week!"

"Have a blessed week, my dear!" Miriam said as she walked into the kitchen to wash her coffee cup.

Bea was smiling as she added Miriam's wisdom to her journal that evening:

Things I've learned from other women:

Kelly White: Be self-aware. Do what makes you happy.

Rhonda Burton: Don't lose yourself in any relationship.

Tamara Humphrey: Stop saying you can't do something—you never know until you try!

Noisha Clark: Focus on your values.

Sheila Cummings: Do not become overly reliant upon the opinions of others, living your life according to what "they" say.

Madeline Fox: Forgiveness—of self and others. Life is all about choices.

Ling Wu: Let go of the shoulds!

Miriam Mavens: Find your passion. Have an "attitude of gratitude."

AWARENESS

Self-awareness: take a look at what makes you happy.

Be aware of what you are giving up or what

you are not even attempting to try.

Values: write them down!

Be aware of your choices.

Do something because it is right for you, not just because someone or something told you that you should do it.

Watch not only what you say, but how you say it.

Find your passion.

ACCEPTANCE

Forgive the judgments you hold on yourself and others.

Find your focus and stick to it.

Accept your humanity.

ABUNDANCE

Accept the wisdom of others.

Have an attitude of gratitude.

CHAPTER 13:
MEETING THE QUEEN BEE

"So, is this the big week?" Velma asked as she filed Bea's nails.

"The big week?" Bea asked, lost in thoughts about all she needed to get done.

"Helloooooo... Earth to Bea! Isn't this the week that Dana Meadows comes to town? Lord, how can something like that slip your mind?!" Velma said, shaking her head.

"Oh, THAT!" Bea answered. "Um, yes. I'm so overwhelmed with everything I have to do that I hardly know what day it is! It isn't like the first time we've done this show, but this will be the first time I'm actually helping to produce it. A little more pressure."

"And a lot more excitement!" Velma said. "Now, we have to make sure you are looking so very fine for when you meet Miss Meadows! Is this the color you want on your nails? No, no, NO! What are you thinking, Sugar?! You need to be classy! Velma's going to do a nice neutral color for you."

"But..." Bea began, and then thought otherwise. There was really no changing Velma's mind when she had an idea of how it should be. She sighed and settled back into the chair. "I'm not so sure I'll be meeting her, Velma. I'm just doing all the behind the scenes stuff, you know."

"Well, you need to be prepared anyway," Velma countered. "Besides, I just have this feeling you're going to meet her. Mark my words. You've been in her energy all this time with your little project!"

Bea smiled. "Well, you never know."

"So, what are you going to say to her when you meet?" Velma asked assuredly.

"Well, IF I meet her, I'll just say... hmmm. I have no idea. It's interesting. Last year when you first suggested to me that I talk to other women about how she does it, I had Dana up on such a high pedestal. She was the 'be all, end all,' the unachievable gold standard. And then, during this process, I realized that there are a LOT of women out there who are the same as her: comfortable in their own skin, knowing who they are and what is important to them, and doing amazing things in their own corner of the world because of it. And Dana Meadows is just one of them! OK, she's a really rich and famous one of them, but I think that is how she got there and stays there: She knows herself and has tapped into that power within her. So, to answer your question, if this was last year, I'd be all tongue-tied and falling all over her. Now, I'm just not sure. My view of her has changed."

Velma stopped and looked at Bea. "No, Sugar, YOU'VE changed."

Bea was shocked. "You think so? In what way?"

Velma continued, "Well, you know how they say it: 'It's your energy.' You are calmer, and more confident. Those little things that used to rattle your cage just seem to slide off your back now. You are more connected to the real Bea. And just like you said about Dana, you seem to have tapped into that power within you. You've got yourself a little of that Dana magic!"

Bea took a moment to let that sink in. "You know, I do feel better about where I am and who I am than I did last year. Well, maybe there IS something to it!" She smiled warmly at Velma. "Thank you so much for your help!"

Velma patted her hand and met her eyes. "It's what I do!" she said with a laugh. "Now go on and get that show on the road, you Superbwoman, you!"

Bea thought about what Velma said as she walked back to work. She HAD changed! And so had her

THE SUPERB WOMAN

life since she started her project. First, she had learned to say 'No.' That was not easy. She thought about the first time she said it, haltingly, when someone asked her to head a PTA committee. They were shocked at her response, as in the past she had always said yes whenever asked to do anything. And while it felt a little awkward that first time, she found that the more she understood what worked for her and what didn't, the easier it was to say no. It had been a huge time saver for her, and had given her back the time and energy she needed for the things that really mattered to her, like her kids.

And speaking of kids, Bea was noticing a change in them as well. As she became more confident and less stressed, so did they. *I guess they do notice me after all,* she mused. While she had always "been there" for them, she realized that not only was she there physically for them, but also now she was really present emotionally as well. And it seemed to make a difference in their relationships—which, with budding teens, became even more important. She smiled at the awareness.

And then there was work. Her meeting with Peggy DeBaar had been the catalyst to her professional growth. Bea had reached back out to Peggy a few weeks after their lunch and asked if she would mind being a mentor to her. Peggy had accepted eagerly, and they had formed a wonderful friendship and working relationship. And when Peggy heard of an opening coming up on the Production team, she had no hesitation in recommending Bea for the job. And Bea had taken Peggy's advice to heart about her languaging, becoming more confident in the way she expressed herself.

And lastly, there was gratitude. Bea reflected on the messages she got from Madeline and Noisha and Ling and Miriam. All had expressed such gratitude for their journeys, even though none had been a cakewalk. Bea had taken to adding a gratitude column in her nightly journal, which helped her observe the good things in her life during the day. Yes, her life had changed and was continuing to evolve in ways she could not have imagined only a year ago. She shook her head and sent up a silent prayer of gratitude as she opened the door to return to her new job, which was about to get even more exciting.

Bea was doing a final walkthrough of the auditorium to make sure all the details were in place for today's rehearsal. As she neared the elevator bank to take her up to the backstage area, she saw Dana

Meadows and her assistant approaching from the other direction. With a deep breath, Bea held the door open for them to join her. "Going up?" she asked.

"Yes, thank you," said the assistant, a woman Bea had been working with on this year's event.

Bea smiled back and caught Dana's eye.

"Hi, I'm Dana," she said, smiling and extending her hand. "Have we met before? You look so familiar..."

Before Bea could answer, her assistant said, "You may have seen her. This is Bea. She's the Superwoman who helps produce the events here."

Bea extended her hand and shook Dana's warmly. "Well, as my friend says, 'One heart recognizes another.' Such a pleasure to meet you!"

"I like that!" Dana replied with a smile.

And with Velma's voice echoing in her head, she added, "And no, I'm not a 'Superwoman.' I prefer to think of myself as a 'Superbwoman'—emphasis on the 'b.' You know, it's all about the BE," she said with a wink, pointing to herself.

"Indeed it is," Dana said with a knowing smile.

ACKNOWLEDGMENTS

The concept of The Superbwoman would never have happened had I not met, and been encouraged by, amazing SUPERB women! From my literal very beginning, the love and support of my mother, grandmother, sisters, aunts, cousins and countless friends has helped guide and embolden me to a place where I am now truly comfortable in my own skin. While I am quite confident I am forgetting key individuals, (and forgive me for that!), let me acknowledge a few that have been of particular guidance in bringing this volume to fruition:

James Savage: A loving man who has supported me and all I do from the moment we met. I literally could not have gone off to write this without him nor would I have the life I have today without his steadfast love.

My children - Timothy (and his wife Jing), Christopher, and Emily all have given me the love and lessons to be a better parent and a better person.

My sisters, Jean and Joan - Both of whom bring me laughter and love and many, many shared adventures!

My parents, Barbara and John - Steadfast in their support and belief in me through it all.

My friends - Too numerous to list, but each holding a special place in my heart.

My college and grad school friends – From Vermont to California, these are the people who saw me at my highest and lowest points, and were there to lift me up.

Wendy Newman – Whose encouragement and creativity helped to create the Superbwoman brand.

Donna Miller – A friend, sometimes boss, always colleague, and great person to laugh with. Her generosity of spirit and resources has brought me through more than one of life's journeys.

The Tribe of Superbwomen – My amazing group who believe in the power of women helping each other!

The women I've interviewed for my web-show, *Superbwomen Sundays at 7* – You are literally the inspiration for the characters in this book. Your stories are rich and warm and heartbreaking and real and very important! Thank you for sharing them with me and our viewers/readers.

The Enlightened Bestseller Workshop leaders and participants - Geoff Affleck, Chris and Janet Attwood, Marci Shimoff helped me to bring my ideas into reality. And my fellow authors who were there for the course: Thank you for being a listening ear and a willing participant in this "birth process". Particular thanks to Dr. John Filo and Magnes Welsh for continuing to be along on this journey, and to Sarah Beckman for her loving kindness!

Joel and Heidi Roberts – Joel's unique laser-focused coaching helped push me out of my comfort zone and into a more authentic place of being. Thank you for your support in this process!

Karen Anderson – Thank you for stopping your car to tell me how much you related to and resonated with my story. That simple act connected us personally and professionally and brought me to a fruition of a dream.

Diane Byrne – This "big picture" gal is forever grateful for people like you who care about the details! Thank you for lovingly editing my copy!

Jan Goldstoff – The Gal with the Golden Rolodex, for her unwavering support, promotion and friendship.

Judy Katz –One conversation with Judy about my idea for this book and she helped me clarify the style and format. Thanks for wisdom and gift!

Morgan James Publishing – What a gift to have been introduced to and to work with a highly competent and equally lovely group of individuals. A special shout-out to Tiffany Gibson, Jim Howard, Nickcole Watkins, and David Hancock, for their professionalism and support through the process.

But most of all, a huge thank you to everyone I continue to meet on my path who bring me life lessons, laughter, and a whole lot of love! May you all realize how truly SUPERB you are!

Morgan James
Speakers Group

www.TheMorganJamesSpeakersGroup.com

We connect Morgan James published authors
with live and online events and audiences who
will benefit from their expertise.

Morgan James makes all of our titles available through the Library
for All Charity Organization.

www.LibraryForAll.org

CPSIA information can be obtained
at www.ICGtesting.com
Printed in the USA
BVHW03s1443180818
524676BV00003B/2